You Are in Ancient Egypt

Ivan Minnis

www.raintreepublishers.co.uk
Visit our website to find out more information about **Raintree** books.

To order:
☎ Phone 44 (0) 1865 888112
▤ Send a fax to 44 (0) 1865 314091
▱ Visit the Raintree Bookshop at **www.raintreepublishers.co.uk** to browse our catalogue and order online.

First published in Great Britain by Raintree, Halley Court, Jordan Hill, Oxford OX2 8EJ, part of Harcourt Education.
Raintree is a registered trademark of Harcourt Education Ltd.

Editorial: Nick Hunter and Catherine Clarke
Design: Michelle Lisseter, Richard Parker and Celia Floyd
Illustrations: Jeff Edwards
Picture Research: Maria Joannou and Ginny Stroud-Lewis
Production: Kevin Blackman

Originated by Dot Gradations Ltd
Printed and bound in China by South China Printing Company

ISBN 1 844 43285 8
08 07 06 05 04
10 9 8 7 6 5 4 3 2 1

British Library Cataloguing in Publication Data
Minnis, Ivan
You are in Ancient Egypt. – (You Are There)
932'.01
A full catalogue record for this book is available from the British Library.

Acknowledgements
The publishers would like to thank the following for permission to reproduce photographs:
AKG Images pp. **5** (Erich Lessing), **8** (Erich Lessing), **11** (Erich Lessing), **12** (Erich Lessing), **17**, **18** (Erich Lessing), **19** (Erich Lessing); Alamy Images (Ian M. Butterfield) p. **22**; Ancient Art and Architecture pp. **6**, **7** (R. Sheridan), **9**, **10** (R. Sheridan), **13** (R. Sheridan), **15**, **23** (R. Sheridan), **24** (J. Stevens), **26** (R. Sheridan), **28** (R. Sheridan); The Ancient Egypt Picture Library pp. **14**, **29**; Peter Evans pp. **4**, **20**, **27**; Phil Cooke and Magnet Harlequin pp. **21**, **25**.

Cover photograph of a carved pharaoh head and obelisk with hieroglyphics, in Luxor, reproduced with permission of James Davis Travel Photography.

Every effort has been made to contact copyright holders of any material reproduced in this book. Any omissions will be rectified in subsequent printings if notice is given to the publishers.

The paper used to print this book comes from sustainable resources.

Contents

A great civilization 4

The ancient Egyptians 6

Egyptian towns 8

Egyptian farms. 10

Food and drink. 12

Growing up 14

Reading and writing 16

Egyptian art 18

Egyptian technology. 20

Pharaohs and law 22

Religious beliefs. 24

Life after death 26

Facts for Ancient Egypt 28

Find out for yourself 30

Glossary. 31

Index 32

Any words appearing in bold, **like this**, are explained in the Glossary.

A great civilization

Around 5000 years ago, great **civilizations** were beginning to appear all over the world. In southern Europe, the Minoan people were building great palaces. In Asia, cities were being built along the valley of the River Indus, in what is now Pakistan.

The strongest of all these great civilizations were the ancient Egyptians. By 2500 BC, the people of Egypt had built many great buildings. We can still see some of them today. The kings, or **pharaohs**, of Egypt became rich and powerful.

N
W E
S

Memphis

River Nile

•Thebes

0 _____ 200 miles
0 _____ 300 kilometres

Ancient
Egypt

AFRICA

This map shows the location of ancient Egypt. Memphis and Thebes were two of the most important cities.

4

The Sphinx was a symbol of royal power. It showed a creature that was half lion, half pharaoh.

Over 3000 years ago, Ramses II ruled Egypt for 67 years. He became so famous and powerful that he is now called Ramses the Great.

The greatest pharaoh

Egypt's power lasted for almost 3000 years. In this book you are going to travel around 3250 years back in time to Egypt at the time of Ramses II, who ruled from 1279 to 1213 BC. He was one of the greatest of all the pharaohs.

The ancient Egyptians

Imagine walking through an ancient-Egyptian town. You can see many different types of people. Rich men and women love fashion and beauty. Poorer people wear clothes that are designed for working hard in the burning sun. You may see some slaves, captured in distant lands by the armies of Ramses II.

Egypt is a very hot country, so people wear light clothes. In this tomb painting, the men are throwing grain in the air to separate the wheat.

Rich and poor

Rich people wear beautiful clothes made of fine **linen**. The women wear valuable jewellery and colourful make-up. Their jewellery is often decorated with coloured stones and pictures of the many Egyptian gods. The men wear eye make-up as well.

Poor people dress very simply. Most men wear just a basic linen **loincloth**. This keeps them cool when working in the hot sun. The women wear simple linen dresses.

Wealthy people wear fine clothes and jewellery.

Finding out about clothes

We know about Egyptian clothes because people have found paintings on Egyptian **tombs** that show what people wore. Clothes and jewellery have also been found in tombs. The Egyptians believed they would need these things in the **afterlife**.

Egyptian towns

Egypt is a desert country. Great cities like Memphis and Thebes are beside the River Nile. You cannot just turn on a tap in ancient Egypt. You and your friends have to walk to the river every day to pick up water for cooking and washing. It is much easier to travel to other cities by boat, rather than across the rough desert land.

Every summer the river floods. Then, farmers and their families have to help to move water from the flood on to the fields. This makes the land **fertile** for growing **crops**.

The land along the banks of the River Nile is very fertile.

Going inside

Your ancient-Egyptian house is probably made of mud bricks and reeds. It has just two or three rooms. Thick walls keep things cool inside. In the evenings, your family will sit on the flat roof. People like to eat and talk there when the sun is not so hot. Rich people's houses are much larger. They may have a garden with a fish pond.

Egyptian farms

When the river floods it brings water and rich, dark mud to the farmers' fields. After the floods the farmers sow their seeds and wait for the **crops** to grow. The main crops grown are barley and a kind of wheat for bread. Farmers also grow **flax**. This is made into **linen** for their clothes. They grow other crops such as dates, grapes, lettuces and onions. Animals are important, too. Oxen pull the heavy **ploughs**. Donkeys carry heavy loads from the fields to the towns.

You might see farmers ploughing their fields with the help of oxen.

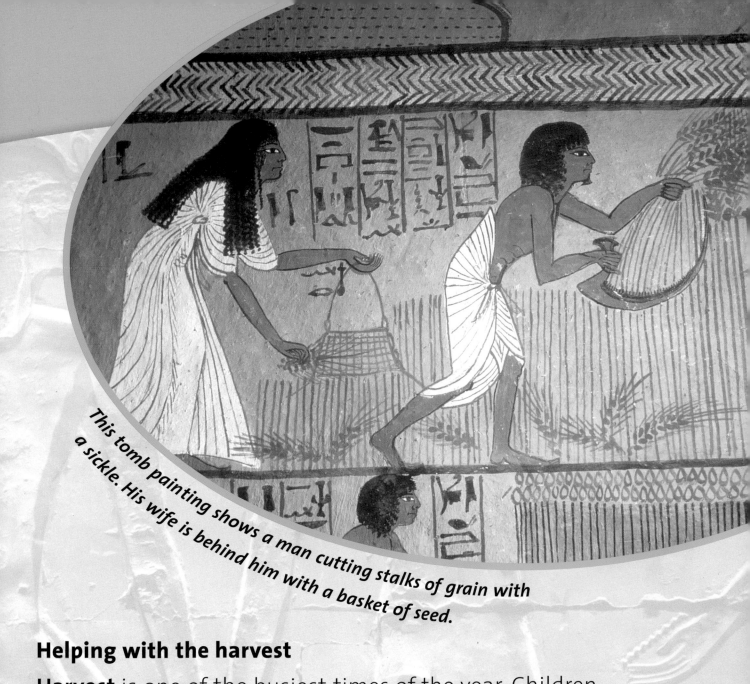

This tomb painting shows a man cutting stalks of grain with a sickle. His wife is behind him with a basket of seed.

Helping with the harvest

Harvest is one of the busiest times of the year. Children like you have to help out. A sharp tool called a sickle is used to harvest the grain. It is loaded on to donkeys and taken to be milled into flour. At the mill you can see **scribes** carefully weighing the grain and recording the amount brought by each farmer. Farmers must all give a share of their crop to the **pharaoh** as a **tax**.

Food and drink

There are no fridges in ancient Egypt. People have to make fresh food every day. They can bring things they have grown themselves to the market to swap, or barter, for other goods.

You eat freshly-baked bread nearly every day. It tastes gritty because the flour is ground on a stone mill. Along with your bread, you may have some vegetables or fruit such as figs or melon. People also eat fish caught in the River Nile. Your meal will be washed down with a drink like beer that is made from barley. This drink is so lumpy you have to drink it through a wooden strainer.

Bread is a very important part of the ancient-Egyptian diet. This model shows a baker grinding corn into flour.

If you go to a feast, you can eat with your fingers. You'll have a knife to cut your food.

Food for the rich

You may be lucky enough to eat with a wealthy family. The rich eat much more meat than the poor. They feast on dishes such as antelope, heron and pelican, as well as roasted pig or sheep. Honey cakes or raisin bread taste sweet, but they will still be gritty and sandy.

Growing up

You and your friends in ancient Egypt do not have much time for playing. Poor children spend most of their lives working hard in the fields with their families. You will have to join in **harvesting** the **crop**. If you are the son of a tradesperson, such as a jeweller or a carpenter, you will learn your father's trade.

Even rich children have a fairly tough life. The boys are sent to school. They start school aged five and can leave to get work by the age of twelve.

Only boys can become scribes and work for the pharaoh. They must work hard and learn to read and write.

Very few girls go to school. They stay at home and learn how to manage the house. Girls marry around the age of fourteen. Their husbands are usually about sixteen years old.

At play

When there is time, you and your friends play many different games. You can play with balls, dolls and toy animals such as horses, dogs and crocodiles.

Finding out about toys

Some toys have been found in the **tombs** of young children. Models of animals were made out of wood and clay. Spinning tops were made from stone, clay or wood.

If you are lucky enough to have time to play, toys like this wooden horse are popular.

Reading and writing

Boys who go to school can learn to become a **scribe**. Scribes are the cleverest men in Egypt. They get the top jobs with the **pharaoh**. They can read and write. Ancient Egyptians write using **hieroglyphs**. The writing is made up of many symbols, or pictures, for different sounds or objects. As a young scribe you will need to learn and remember over 700 symbols.

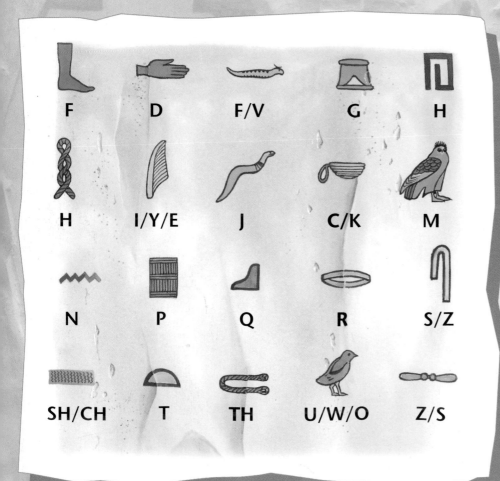

F	D	F/V	G	H
H	I/Y/E	J	C/K	M
N	P	Q	R	S/Z
SH/CH	T	TH	U/W/O	Z/S

Here are some of the symbols you might learn in ancient Egypt.

Finding out about hieroglyphs

For thousands of years, people did not know how to read hieroglyphs. Then, in 1799, the Rosetta Stone was found. It had writing in hieroglyphs as well as in Greek. Because people could read Greek, they could work out the hieroglyphs. They could then read other Egyptian writing in carvings, on papyrus and on wall paintings.

Many pieces of papyrus have beautiful pictures and hieroglyphs on them.

Paper and ink

The scribes write on a kind of paper called **papyrus**. It is made from the reeds that grow along the banks of the Nile. Reeds are also used as pens, with ink made from charcoal or soot.

17

Egyptian art

As you travel around ancient Egypt you will see art everywhere. You do not need to visit an art gallery. It is painted on the walls of temples, palaces and public buildings. Some of the best art is hidden away inside the **tombs** of the great **pharaohs**. No one can see this art once the tomb is sealed up. It will help the pharaoh in the **afterlife**.

Once the tomb is sealed, no one can see the paintings.

Egyptian artists always draw people in the same way. Their heads are seen from the side and their bodies from the front and side. Brushes are made from reeds. Plants and **minerals** mixed with water make paints in many beautiful colours. Everyone **respects** artists because they are so skilful. Their art is very important to ancient-Egyptian religion.

Finding out about sculptures

The ancient Egyptians carved many stone statues and figures. Some are huge, like the statues of Ramses II built near the Nile.

There are no cameras in ancient Egypt. Important people are remembered by paintings or statues of themselves.

Egyptian technology

Most people live in one or two-storey houses. The palaces, temples and statues of Egypt tower above these houses. The ancient Egyptians have no machines or cranes. How do they build these huge **monuments**?

Hundreds of people work together to make these great buildings. Farmers and other ordinary people work for the **pharaoh** on his great building projects. Craftsmen use simple tools like hammers, chisels and saws to cut stone blocks. These blocks are then dragged by the workers to slowly create huge buildings. It is very hard work, especially in the hot sun.

Even at the time of Ramses II, this pyramid is over 1000 years old. It was built around 2500 BC.

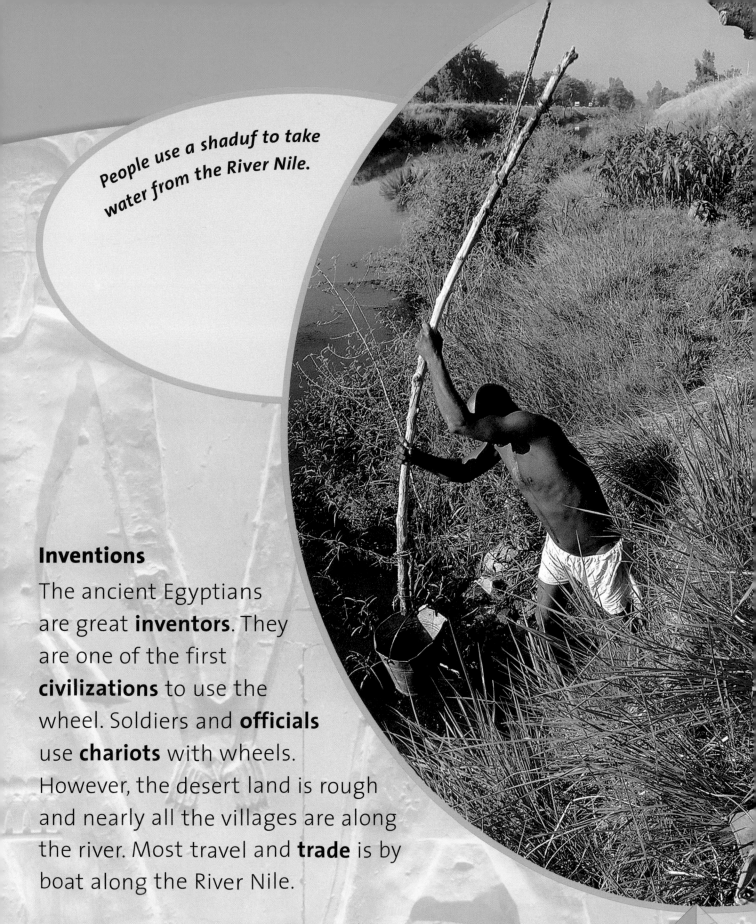

People use a shaduf to take water from the River Nile.

Inventions

The ancient Egyptians are great **inventors**. They are one of the first **civilizations** to use the wheel. Soldiers and **officials** use **chariots** with wheels. However, the desert land is rough and nearly all the villages are along the river. Most travel and **trade** is by boat along the River Nile.

21

Pharaohs and law

Egypt is ruled by a **pharaoh**. As well as being king, the people think he is a god. He has complete power over his people and owns most of the land in Egypt. The pharaoh has many palaces around the country.

Hatshepsut

The most famous pharaohs

▲ Hatshepsut (1472–1458 BC) was a famous female pharaoh. She was supposed to hand the throne to her stepson, but she ended up ruling Egypt for twenty years. She even wore the pharaoh's **ceremonial** beard!

▲ Tutankhamun (1333–1323 BC) was only nine years old when he became pharaoh. He is very famous because of the beautiful treasures found in his **tomb**.

▲ Ramses II (1279–1213 BC) is called Ramses the Great because he was a great warrior. He ruled Egypt for 67 years. It is said he had 96 sons and 60 daughters!

*The pharaoh's **scribes** note down everything that is **harvested**.*
This makes it easier to collect taxes.

Very few ordinary people ever see the pharaoh. You will
have to follow the orders of the local noblemen who
control your village. They have to report to **officials** who
work for the pharaoh. These men collect the **taxes** and
supervise the great building projects. This allows the
pharaoh to make sure his orders are followed.

Religious beliefs

Everyone in ancient Egypt shares the same religious beliefs. They believe that the world is ruled by many different gods. Each god has its own temples. The temples are cared for by priests, who give **offerings** to keep the gods happy. Ordinary people are not allowed inside. Your house has a **shrine** in it. This is so your family can make offerings to the gods who will protect them.

Everyone goes to the temple to celebrate festivals. Only the priests can go inside.

Gods and Goddesses

🔺 Amon-Re was the king of the gods. He was the main god of the city of Thebes. People believed he protected Egypt from its enemies.

🔺 Osiris was the god of the dead. He was also the god of the **Underworld**.

🔺 Isis was the wife of Osiris and was worshipped as the mother goddess.

Re, god of the Sun.

Osiris

The gods and goddesses have temples all over Egypt. People pray to them for help with all sorts of everyday things.

25

Life after death

The ancient Egyptians make great preparations for funerals. Rich men have **tombs** built for their families. The tombs are beautifully painted with pictures of gods and goddesses and scenes of daily life.

After death, the body has its insides removed. Then the body is covered with a salt-like powder called **natron**. After 70 days, the body has dried out and is wrapped in bandages. This is called mummification. Once the mummy is wrapped it can last for thousands of years. The ancient Egyptians believe that the dead person will need their body in the **afterlife**.

Mummies are often buried in beautiful cases.

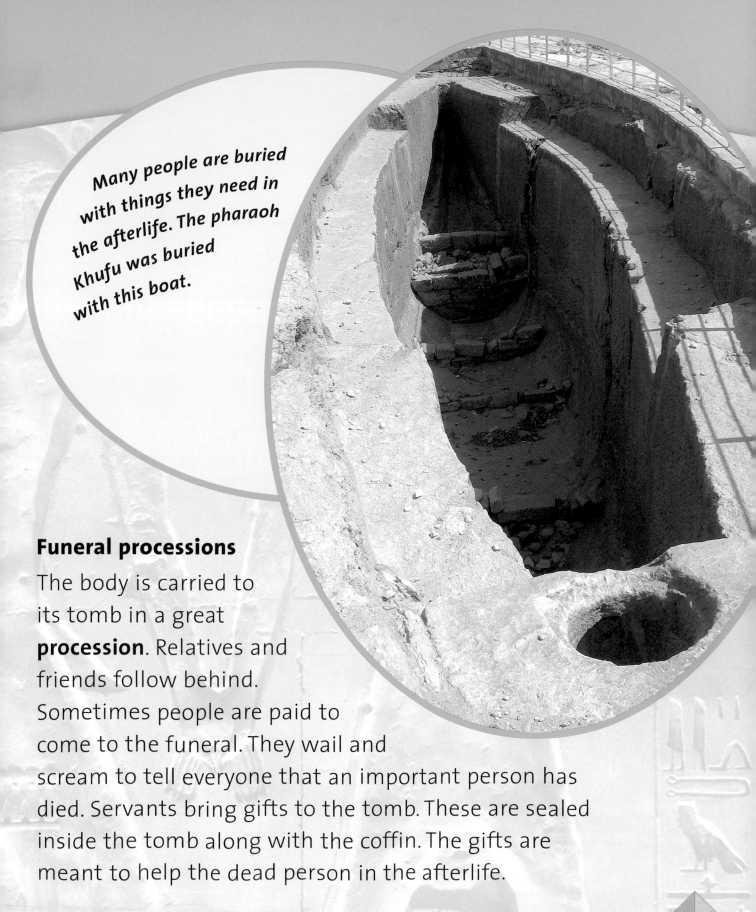

Many people are buried with things they need in the afterlife. The pharaoh Khufu was buried with this boat.

Funeral processions

The body is carried to its tomb in a great **procession**. Relatives and friends follow behind. Sometimes people are paid to come to the funeral. They wail and scream to tell everyone that an important person has died. Servants bring gifts to the tomb. These are sealed inside the tomb along with the coffin. The gifts are meant to help the dead person in the afterlife.

Facts for Ancient Egypt

Now you know a bit about ancient Egypt and its people. Here are a few things you need to know to get by in ancient Egypt:

Time

◆ There are 365 days in the ancient-Egyptian calendar. A new year begins around the time of the Nile flood every year.

◆ Each week lasts for ten days. Builders work for ten days at a time, with one day off.

Crops can be bartered, or swapped, for goods the farmers cannot make themselves.

Money

There is no money in ancient Egypt. Workers are often paid in wheat or barley. To buy things they do not have, ancient Egyptians have to barter, or swap, them for other things.

Dates to remember:

- ◢ around 3000 BC Egypt is united under King Menes

- ◢ around 2600 BC: Great Pyramid built at Giza

- ◢ 1323 BC: the boy-king Tutankhamun is buried in the Valley of the Kings

- ◢ 30 BC: Egypt becomes part of the Roman Empire.

Scales are used by shopkeepers to weigh out their goods.

Numbers

Here are the symbols used for ancient Egyptian numbers:

29

Find out for yourself

Unfortunately, you cannot travel back in time to ancient Egypt, but you can still find out lots about the ancient Egyptians and how they lived. You will find the answers to some of your questions in this book. You can also use other books and the Internet.

Books to read

Ancient Egypt: Sticker Book, Mark Hillsden (Dorling Kindersley, 2000)

History Starts Here: The Ancient Egyptians, Jane Shuter (Hodder Wayland, 2002)

The World of: Egyptian Pharaoh, Anne Millard (Hodder Wayland, 1998)

Using the Internet

Explore the Internet to find out more about ancient Egypt. Websites can change, but if one of the links below no longer works, don't worry. Use a search engine such as www.yahooligans.com, and type in keywords such as 'Tutankhamun', 'mummy', '**pyramids**' and 'ancient Egypt'.

Websites

http://www.pbs.org/wgbh/nova/egypt/explore
Explore ancient Egypt on this interactive site.
http://www1.thdo.bbc.co.uk/history/ancient/egyptians/mummy_maker_game.shtml
Step into the embalmer's workshop when you play this mummy maker game!

Disclaimer
All the Internet addresses (URLs) given in this book were valid at the time of going to press. However, due to the dynamic nature of the Internet, some addresses may have changed, or sites may have ceased to exist since publication. While the author and publishers regret any inconvenience this may cause readers, no responsibility for any such changes can be accepted by either the author or the publishers.

Glossary

afterlife   life that begins after death. The ancient Egyptians believed this was like real life, but perfect.

ceremonial   used for ceremonies

chariot   two-wheeled vehicle pulled by horses

civilization   united group of people living together

crops   plants grown in large amounts, usually for food

fertile   good for growing crops

flax   crop grown for making linen cloth

harvest   gathering together of the crops for the year

hieroglyph   pictures and symbols used instead of letters to mean words

invent   make or discover something for the first time

linen   cloth made from flax

loincloth   piece of clothing worn around the hips

mineral   natural, solid substance

monument   structure built to remind people of an event or special person

natron   mineral used for preserving bodies

offerings   gifts to the gods of animals or other goods

official   important person who works for the pharaoh

papyrus   paper-like material made from papyrus reeds

pharaoh   ruler of the ancient Egyptians

plough   large farming tool, often pulled by animals. Ploughs churn up the soil ready for planting crops.

procession   group of people moving forward together, often as part of a special ceremony

pyramid   huge tombs made from stone with a square base and triangular sides that join at one point

respect   to honour or look up to another person

scribe   person who could read and write and was employed to do so

shrine   special place which is thought to be holy

tax   forced payment to the government for running a country

tomb   place where someone is buried

trade   buying and selling of things

Underworld   place where, according to the ancient Egyptians, a person's spirit goes after death

Index

afterlife 7, 18, 26, 27
Amon-Re 25
animals 10, 15
art 18–19

barter 28
bread 10, 12, 13

calendar 28
chariots 21
children 11, 14–15
clothes 6, 7
craftsmen 14, 20
crops 10, 14

farming 8, 10–11, 14, 20
floods 8, 10, 28
food and drink 12–13
funerals 27

games and toys 15
girls and women 7, 15
gods and goddesses 24, 25, 26

harvest 11, 14, 23
Hatshepsut 22
hieroglyphs 16–17
houses 9, 20

inventions 21
Isis 25
jewellery 7

linen 7, 10

make-up 7
marriage 15

Memphis 4, 8
money 28
mummification 26

numbers 29

Osiris 25

papyrus 17
pharaohs 4, 5, 11, 14, 16, 18, 20, 22–23
poor people 6, 7, 14
pyramids 20, 29

Ramses II 5, 19, 22
reading and writing 16–17
religious beliefs 24–25
rich people 6, 7, 9, 13, 14, 26
River Nile 8, 12, 21

schools 14, 16
scribes 11, 14, 16, 17, 23
sculptures 19
slaves 6

taxes 11, 23
technology 20–21
temples 24, 25
Thebes 4, 8, 25
tomb paintings 6, 7, 11, 13, 18, 26, 28
tombs 15, 18, 26, 27
Tutankhamun 22, 29

Underworld 25

wheel 21

Titles in the *You Are There* series include:

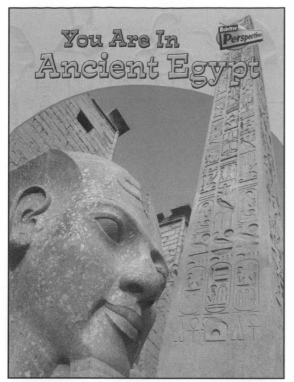

Hardback   1 844 43285 8

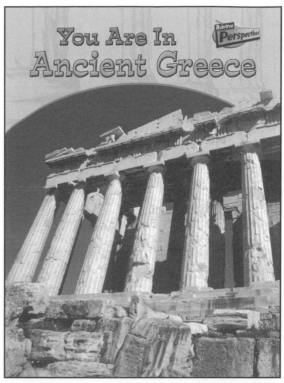

Hardback   1 844 43286 6

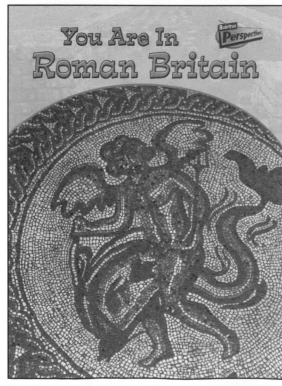

Hardback   1 844 43287 4

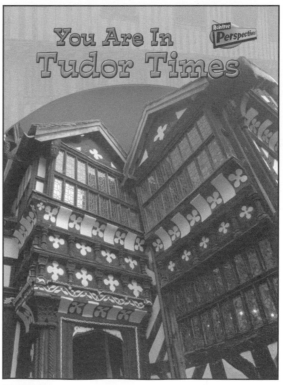

Hardback   1 844 43288 2

Find out about the other titles in this series on our website www.raintreepublishers.co.uk